The Life and Work of...

Pablo Picasso

Leonie Bennett

Heinemann
LIBRARY

H www.heinemann.co.uk/library
Visit our website to find out more information about Heinemann Library books.

To order:
☎ Phone 44 (0) 1865 888066
📄 Send a fax to 44 (0) 1865 314091
💻 Visit the Heinemann Bookshop at www.heinemann.co.uk/library to browse our catalogue and order online.

First published in Great Britain by Heinemann Library, Halley Court, Jordan Hill, Oxford OX2 8EJ, part of Harcourt Education.

Editorial: Nancy Dickmann and Tanvi Rai
Design: Ron Kamen and Celia Jones
Illustrations: Maureen Gray
Picture research: Mica Brancic
Production: Séverine Ribierre

Originated by Repro Multi Warna
Printed and bound by South China Printing Company, China

ISBN 0 431 09326 1 (hardback)
08 07 06 05
10 9 8 7 6 5 4 3 2 1

ISBN 0 431 09333 4 (paperback)
09 08 07 06
10 9 8 7 6 5 4 3 2 1

British Library Cataloguing in Publication Data
Bennett, Leonie
  The life and work of Pablo Picasso
  759.6
A full catalogue record for this book is available from the British Library.

Acknowledgements
The Publishers would like to thank the following for permission to reproduce photographs: AKG pp. 6, 10; AKG/Succession Picasso/DACS 2004 pp. 7, 17, 25; Bridgeman Art Library/Lauros/Giraudon/Museum of Modern Art, New York/ Succession Picasso/DACS 2004 p. 27; Bridgeman Art Library/Metropolitan Museum of Art /DACS 2004 p. 13; Bridgeman Art Library/Private Collection/Succession Picasso/DACS 2004 p. 5; Bridgeman Art Library/ Roger-Viollet/Succession Picasso/DACS 2004 p. 18; Bridgeman Art Library/ The Barnes Foundation Merion, Pennsylvania/Succession Picasso/ DACS 2004 p. 11; Corbis/Bettmann p. 4, 22; Corbis/Francis G. Mayer/ Succession Picasso/ DACS 2004 pp. 9, 21; Corbis/Kimbell Art Museum/Succession Picasso/ DACS 2004 p. 15; Hulton Getty pp. 24, 26; RMN-Beatrice Hatala/Succession Picasso/DACS 2004 p. 19; RMN-Michele Bellot/Succession Picasso/DACS 2004 p. 20; V&A Picture Library C.15-1958/Succession Picasso/DACS 2004 p. 23.

Cover painting (*Las Meninas (after Valazquez 1656 portrait of family of Philip IV of Spain)*, 1957) reproduced with permission of The Art Archive/Succession Picasso/DACS 2004 and portrait of Picasso reproduced with permission of Corbis © Hulton-Deutsch Collection.

Contents

Any words appearing in the text in bold, **like this**, are explained in the Glossary.

Who was Pablo Picasso?

Pablo Picasso was the most famous artist of the 20th century. He was Spanish but he spent most of his life in France.

Pablo Picasso was a painter, **sculptor** and **potter**. He made thousands of works of art and created many different **styles**. This **cubist** picture has simple lines and blocks of colour.

The Red Armchair, 1931

Early years

Pablo Picasso was born in Malaga, Spain, on 25th October 1881. Pablo's father was a painter. Before Pablo could talk he drew pictures to tell people what he wanted.

When Pablo was only ten years old he went to art school. Pablo painted this picture when he was fifteen. His father was the **model** for the doctor.

Science and Charity, 1897

The blue period

Between 1901 and 1904 Pablo spent a lot of time in Paris. A friend died and Picasso became very unhappy. He was also sad because he missed Spain.

Pablo's sadness showed in his art at this time.
He painted people who had difficult lives.
He used the colour blue a lot. This is called his
blue **period**.

The Tragedy,
1903

9

The rose period

In 1904 Pablo met a young woman called
Fernande in Paris. He was happy with her.
Now it was his happiness that showed through
in his paintings.

*Acrobat and
Young
Harlequin*,
1905

Pablo began to use pink in his paintings. This is
called his rose **period**. He loved the circus and
often went three times a week. He liked to
paint circus people.

Masks and statues

Pablo became interested in masks and statues from Africa and South America. He spent a lot of time studying them in museums. They were called **primitive art**.

Pablo sometimes painted people with mask-like faces. He painted a **portrait** of his friend, an American writer called Gertrude. She bought many of Pablo's paintings.

Portrait of Gertrude Stein, 1906

A new style of painting

Pablo began to work closely with another artist called Georges Braque. They tried to paint things from all sides at once. They called this new **style** 'cubism'.

In a cubist picture there are clues to what is shown. If you look carefully at this picture you can see a moustache, an eye, a pipe and some fingers.

Man with a Pipe, 1911

15

Collage

Cubism was very **abstract**. It was hard to recognize the people or objects in the pictures. So Pablo and Georges added things from everyday life to give people clues.

They started making **collages**. They used newspaper headlines, sheet music and bits of wallpaper in their pictures. No one had thought of making works of art like this before.

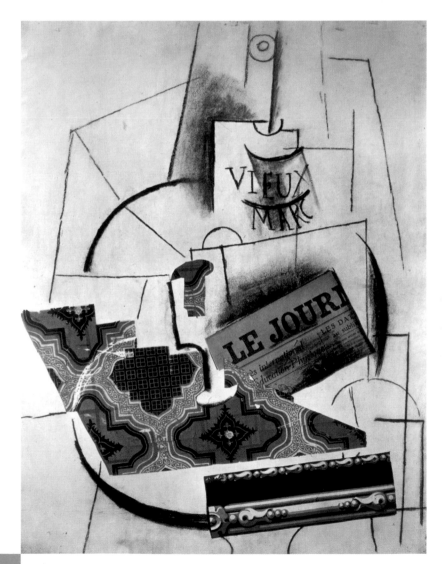

Bottle Vieux Marc, glass and paper, 1913

A new type of sculpture

Pablo made **sculpture** from things he found. At the time this was very unusual. He went for walks and brought back bits of junk that he stored in his studio.

Pablo put together different objects to make new shapes and forms. This bull's head is made from a bicycle saddle and some handlebars.

Bull's Head, 1941

War in Spain

In 1936 a **civil war** began in Spain. Pablo painted pictures to show how he felt about it. Here he is working on the most famous – *Guernica*. It was 8 metres long.

Terrible things were happening to the people of Spain. Pablo painted this picture of a woman crying. It shows us how angry and unhappy he was.

Weeping Woman, 1937

The potter

In 1947 Pablo went to live in the south of France. He had a new **partner** – Françoise – and they had two children, Claude (in picture) and Paloma. Pablo began a new type of work.

Pablo began to make **pottery**. He enjoyed it. In one year he made over 2000 pottery objects. A lot of it was funny like this one.

Mounted Cavalier, 1951

An active old age

In his 70s and 80s, Pablo was still making things and painting pictures. At the end of his life he painted three or four pictures a day.

Pablo had a new **model** named Jacqueline who **inspired** him. In 1961, aged 80, he married her. He painted this **portrait** of her.

Jacqueline with flowers, 1954

Pablo dies

Pablo died on 8 April 1973. He was 91 years old. He left us thousands of works of art. Many famous artists who followed have learnt from him.

Lots of Pablo's work tells how he feels. Some of it is sad. Some of it is angry. But lots of it is happy, like this picture of three musicians.

Three Masked Musicians, 1921

Timeline

1881	Pablo Ruiz Picasso is born on 25 October in Malaga, Spain.
1892	Pablo goes to art school at La Coruna.
1895	Pablo goes to art school in Barcelona.
1897	Pablo enters the Royal Academy, in Madrid. He paints *Science and Charity*.
1901	Pablo visits Paris. The beginning of Pablo's blue **period**.
1903	Pablo paints *The Tragedy*.
1904	Pablo settles in Paris and meets Fernande.
1905	The beginning of Pablo's rose period. Pablo paints *Acrobat* and *Young Harlequin*.
1906	Pablo paints ***Portrait*** of Gertrude Stein.
1907	Pablo meets Georges Braque and they begin to develop **cubism**.
1911	Pablo paints *Man with a Pipe*.
1913	Pablo makes collage *Bottle Vieux Marc, glass and paper*.
1914	The First World War begins.
1918	Pablo marries a Russian dancer called Olga. The First World War ends.
1921	Pablo paints *Three Masked Musicians*.
1925	Pablo takes part in the first **Surrealist** exhibition.
1931	Pablo paints *The Red Armchair*.
1936	The Spanish **Civil War** begins.

1937	Pablo paints *Guernica* and *Weeping Woman*.
1939	The Spanish Civil War ends.
	The Second World War begins. Pablo spends most of it in Paris.
1941	Pablo makes the **sculpture** *Bull's Head*.
1945	The Second World War ends.
1947	Pablo goes to live in the south of France and makes lots of **pottery**.
1951	Pablo makes the pottery figure *Mounted Cavalier*.
1954	Pablo paints a portrait of Jacqueline Roque, called *Jacqueline with flowers*.
1961	Pablo marries Jacqueline.
1973	Pablo dies on 8 April.

Glossary

abstract art that explores ideas rather than the way things look

civil war war between people of the same country

collage picture made with paper, wood or other materials as well as paint

cubism style of painting that shows objects from all sides at once

Guernica town in northern Spain which was badly bombed in 1937

inspire to help someone to be creative

model person who the artist draws or paints

partner person one lives with as if they were a husband or wife

period an amount of time

portrait a picture of a person

potter someone who makes things from clay, usually pots

primitive art art of native people of Africa, Latin America and the Pacific, often made for religious reasons

sculptor an artist who makes art which is not flat - often made of wood, stone or metal

sculpture a piece of art made by a sculptor

style way in which a thing looks

surrealist an artist who does work that is dream-like, using objects in an unexpected way

Find out more

More books to read

Picasso and the Girl with a Ponytail: A Story of Pablo Picasso, Laurence Anholt ed. (Frances Lincoln, 1998)

Life Times: The Story of Pablo Picasso, Liz Gogerly (Belitha Press, 2003)

Adventures in Art: A Day with Picasso, Susanne Pfleger (Prestel Publishing, 1999)

More paintings to see

Les Demoiselles d'Avignon, Metropolitan Museum of Art, New York

Guernica, Reina Sophia, Madrid

Head of a Woman, Tate, Liverpool

Bowl of Fruit, Violin and Bottle, Tate Modern, London

The Old Guitarist, Art Institute, Chicago

Websites to visit

http://www.picasso.com
Packed with information about Picasso's life and times and also has a gallery with many paintings on display.

http://www.enchantedlearning.com/artists/picasso
Contains outlines of Picasso paintings that can be printed out and coloured in.

Index